\blak\ \al-fə bet

ABOUT THE LEXI RUDNITSKY
EDITOR'S CHOICE AWARD

The Lexi Rudnitsky Editor's Choice Award is a collaboration between Persea Books and The Lexi Rudnitsky Poetry Project. It sponsors the annual publication of a poetry collection by an American who has published at least once previous full-length book of poems. The Editor's Choice Award is the second collaboration between Persea and the Lexi Rudnitsky Poetry Project, following the Lexi Rudnitsky First Book Prize in Poetry, awarded annually to an American woman who has yet to publish a book. Both awards are conducted via contest. Entry guidelines are available on Persea's website.

Lexi Rudnitsky (1972–2005) grew up outside of Boston, and studied at Brown University and Columbia University. Her own poems exhibit both a playful love of language and a fierce conscience. Her writing appeared in *The Antioch Review, Columbia: A Journal of Literature and Art, The Nation, The New Yorker, The Paris Review, Pequod*, and *The Western Humanities Review*. In 2004, she won the Milton Kessler Memorial Prize for Poetry from *Harpur Palate*.

Lexi died suddenly in 2005, just months after the birth of her first child and the acceptance for publication of her first book of poems, *A Doorless Knocking into Night* (Mid-List Press, 2006). The Lexi Rudnitsky book prizes were created to memorialize her by promoting the type of poet and poetry in which she so spiritedly believed.

\ˈblak\\ˈal-fə̩bet\

POEMS

Mitchell L.H. Douglas

Winner of the 2011 Lexi Rudnitsky Editor's Choice Award

A Karen & Michael Braziller Book
PERSEA BOOKS / NEW YORK

Persea Books, Inc.
277 Broadway
New York, NY 10007

Library of Congress Cataloging-in-Publication Data
Douglas, Mitchell L. H., 1970—
\blak\ \al-fe bet\ : poems / Mitchell L.H. Douglas.—First edition.
    pages cm
Includes bibliographical references.
"Winner of the 2011 Lexi Rudnitsky Editor's Choice Award."
ISBN 978-0-89255-421-8 (original trade pb : alk. paper)
I. Title.

PS3604.O9323B53 2013
811'.6—dc23
    2012042828

First edition
Printed in the United States of America
Designed by Rita Lascaro

For Mamie Lee Green. I miss you with an ache.

Contents

\blak\ \al-fə bet

COFFER

Lord, loose this blues,
throb of bruise encased
in coffer.

I am a man of grave undoing.

The month is June,
but nothing blooms. Our matriarch
Mamie Lee — Southern aura —
gives up the ghost, plows
our hearts. Knees bent
to hospital hallways,
we wail w/out conscience,
no hand to catch the trail,
infinite stream:
face submerged, body
unhinged.
      Tubes & needles
catapult the beat of hearts, erode
bravado. Thy kingdom
come, thy will be done. Who
will right this fall?

Your names, please. Your names.

Keep wringing your hands,
keep a spade close
to your heart, hold fast
& in night's demise
think: dig. When the spirit

flies the coffer,
dear father, what
is our portion?

Who is barren
& who coin?

I. allegiance

"For I am rightful fellow of their band.
My best allegiances are to the dead."

—GWENDOLYN BROOKS

CERTIFICATE OF BIRTH
STATE OF ALABAMA—BUREAU OF VITAL STATISTICS

File No. for State Registrar Only.
129200

PLACE OF BIRTH

STATE BOARD OF HEALTH
Reg. District or
Beat No. _240012_ Certificate No._____

County _Dallas_

Town or City _Selma_

Street or R.F.D._____ Ward_____

(If birth occurred in a hospital or institution, give its NAME instead of street and number)

Full Name of Child _George Washington Green_

If child is not yet named, make supplemental report when named.

| BOY OR GIRL _Boy_ | To be answered ONLY in event of plural births | 4 Twin, triplet or other_____ 5 Number, in order of birth_____ | (6) Are Parents Maried? _yes_ | (7) DATE OF BIRTH _Feb 23_ 192 _5_ (Name of Month) (Day) (Year) |

FATHER

FULL NAME _George Green_

PRESENT POSTOFFICE OF FATHER _Tyler_

COLOR OR RACE _colored_ (11) AGE AT LAST BIRTHDAY _23_ (Years)

BIRTHPLACE _Dallas Co._

OCCUPATION _Farmer_

Number of children born to Mother, including present birth)_____

MOTHER

(14) NAME BEFORE MARRIAGE _Lola Bissel_

(15) PRESENT POSTOFFICE OF MOTHER _Tyler_

(16) COLOR OR RACE _colored_ (17) AGE AT LAST BIRTHDAY _19_ (Years)

(18) BIRTHPLACE _Dallas Co._

(19) OCCUPATION _Farm Wife_

(21) Number of children of this mother now living, including present birth)_____

CERTIFICATE OF ATTENDING PHYSICIAN OR MIDWIFE*

I hereby certify that I attended the birth of this child, who was born _alive_ at _7 p.m._
on the date above stated.   (Alive or Stillborn)   (Hour A.M. or P.M.)

(23) Signature _Maria Green_

(24) State whether Physician or Midwife) _midwife_

(25) Address of Physician or Midwife) _Tyler_

(26) Witness _____
(Signature of Witness necessary only when question 21 is signed by mark)

(27) Filed _Mar 4_ 192 _5_ (28) _Mrs. E. A. Poole_
Local Registrar

HOUSETOP
(for Matilda Gohagan)

Through daylight, through denim,
nightfall and sunflower,
through parched grass, through violets,
melon rind, melon flesh,
you sew a plow's winding path—
loving turn of earth.

I leave Selma, filled
with proof of fingers' work,
how we weave love
into a soft, warming field.
From the center out, heart
built on the strength of seed,
yield of crop,
raising fences in honor
arms interlocked
holding in, not keeping out.

When I board the train back,
I wrap our stories around me,
think of the stitches—
the way a bloodline is born,
the way we honor the art.

ALABAMA, 1976

Met America in an observation car
long before I knew a history book—
her stories raced down
southbound rails, tales by passengers

& porters, first class to coach.
In the bubble of an Amtrak
destined for Birmingham,
I sat with Granddaddy,

saw barbed wire & tobacco barns
pulled west to east like film advancing.
A height where people
are too close to be ants, air

too rich to gasp. A wanderer's view,
our windows open to home.

THIRD EYE

Consider yourself woven & see
what your gut says: voice

frayed in scratch, swift pulse,
knot stomach. Recall

the hour you saw yourself alive,
out of body—when three dimensional

became epiphany, like the first time
you did anything. Today, you explain

ways your eyes spied heaven,
shot back down, saw yourself

pot bellied & Afro'd. Aged in single digits,
you talked to cousins in the middle room

where Mamie Lee burned cigarettes
instead of smoking

& soap operas played endlessly,
stories no child

disclosed. Consider yourself
stitch, soft thread

that ties one tale to next.
Find niche   hover,

trust sixth sense
gifts scenes to spill. Cacophony,

harmony — be owner. Open
your mouth; spin yarn to breath.

BOP: OHIO RIVER/RIVER CITY

At the bottom, rumor has it,
is Ali's gold medal
likely nestled
next to wayward tractors,
slave shackles, & rusted
forget-me-nots of the '37 flood.

I jumped in the river
& what did I see?
Black-eyed angels
swam w/me.

City sips a steady diet
of liquid metal, faithful
citizens lining vital organs
w/gold dust tea, flakes
of oxidized orange
coating mason jar floors
like sugar grains
in libations (too sweet).

Jumped in the river
& what did I see?
Black-eyed angels
swam w/me.

At the bottom, rumor has it:
forget-me-nots of the '37 flood.
Is Ali's gold medal
slave shackles, & rusted

likely nestled
next to wayward tractors?

Jumped
into the river.
Black-eyed angels
swam w/me.

HOOD

In memory of smokestack lighting, red brick wall & wait, graffiti buzz scrawled high & wrong, the misspelled misrepresented; in sweet run sour, endless slabs of cement, bath of street lamp, gutter litter, alley to alley end zone, BB gun aim, tree climb, bird's eye view, calls ignored for lunch, for supper (sorry, too busy in branches); in the wake of Uncle Buddy's fist & forearm through side door glass, ambulance on our would-be 50 yard line, suture map of fold & tuck, flesh envelope. *No need for meds*, he thinks, *I'm fine* (never mind the call to swallow); in contempt of stilted tongue, shuttle black alphabets like lost blood—L&N wind & lash, KY to TN—or skip prattle like hopscotch grids in lime, lemon, pink electric—asphalt body rock—until there is no curb between street & skin—warm, black, waved.

AL GREEN WAS A PREACHER

before he was a pastor—
let me explain. If you can't find
a sermon in "Love & Happiness,"
something's wrong. He slides
from one strange world to the next
like Uncle Jimmy navigating his sky blue Cougar
down West Market. Al testifies
& we glide, past the Coffee Cup,
where we ate greasy burgers
in white paper, the ring & sugar
of onions steamed inside. Past
Jay's, where momma bought my black
Chuck Taylors for first grade. Past
the Cavalier Inn, a bar
only a biker could love, peeling paint
& look-away faces. Past the Laundromat
where Daddy George washed our clothes
in big chrome troughs that ate our change,
bleached our robes.

Al would know this world, would sing
of the corners' jut to meet you,
the pain of the angle, how one street
runs right into the next, no one
raising eyebrows. We ride deeper west, rising
out of our seats and settling back to the cushions
with each pock in the road. Past St. Columba
where I bloodied Jay's nose in the lunch line.
Best friend, how many times
can I say I'm sorry? Past Shawnee

where Momma, Aunt Sissy, and Uncle Jimmy
said high school is not enough. Past
empty Nehi bottles, bodies
of cigarettes bent in gutters,
what smoldered in the grip of unknown lips
discarded for other pleasures.

Many a lesson waits
on our streets, like how to catch
lightning bugs in mayonnaise jars,
how to poke holes in lids
to let trophies breathe. How
to balance your weight
on two bicycle wheels,
never fall, ride
like the unfettered skip
of your heart.

GUIDING STAR MISSIONARY BAPTIST CHURCH
(Rev. E. E. Heard, Pastor)

Rev. Heard half preaches, half
sings, hoists a microphone

with his left hand, hops back on the good foot,
his right. He screams *I'm glad*

no matter the sermon,
what amens & hallelujahs

already spent. He opens his palms
like sacrificial wounds, sighs

The doors of the church are open.

Deacons crowd the pulpit, a fist
of petals, fall out of formation

like a morning bloom. Rev. Heard
repeats the call, six hands

& six sets of eyes willing any sinner
to walk the aisle, for God

to trouble the water. The church
ignores the call & the choir,

one slick muscle, opens its throat, throws
"I Know I Been Changed"

at the ceiling's bare beams. Now:
some brave soul, hands fresh from the hem,

will rise from the back pew, stride toward the flock—
hands still extended, eyes still calling—answer

Yes. I will wade.

II. fire, defy

*"The image is fire
blackening the vague lines
into defiance"*

—AUDRE LORDE

SECOND CHILD

Does this explain the heart? How
one finds another, families
intertwined like crops

on farms standing root to root.
John & Matilda's second born,
George & Leola's second star—

miles traveled
to find the beat. Selma bred
& wilting in all its heat,

longing for the North
to cool the edge. Nine mouths
raised on beans & cornbread;

a living grinding
bathtubs at American Standard;
namesakes sent to college

when you only finished sixth grade.
Graduations, grandchildren,
heart attack, stroke, how one

saves space in the bed years after
the other is called home. No one
loves like this anymore, none dare
fault the heart.

PORCH

The Allens always ate outside. Forget
kitchen, dining room, have a seat
on the porch, listen to the crack
of wood as you find your space,

meditate on a forkful of something hot
& homemade. What good
is a table, square
of silence, meeting of worn faces,

after a day's pull & sweat?
Lawn chairs & steps
are your longing, June's humid kiss
against your cheek, a smile

& wave from your neighbor
as you balance a plate in your lap,
relish ceremony, return
courtesy. Forget

      third shift pays more, overtime
is hard to come by, the fear
of falling short. Your eyes are filled
with familiar hands, lifelines

with the same forks, calluses
you could own.

On the First Drive-by

my family of five packs "the brown tank,"
four-door fortress— a Ford not made any more.
On a Sunday cruise, a car passes, wide tires,
white hide, like the General Lee, bleached.
Every seat filled: a wizard at the wheel,
a shotgun lookout & two backseat drivers
ready to spit & roll, throw sharp tongues
from soiled mouths to scream

      niggers.

      Mother & father
can't bring themselves to speak,
brother & sister my bone flesh
bookends. Our car keeps rolling,
no hum, like the engine is scared
to burn.
   There will be reruns,
without Uncle Jesse,
Bo & Luke,
or a Waylon Jennings soundtrack—
   strangers who won't visit
via TV, a word in rage
until the last ear is gouged.

HOUSETOP VARIATION

Through daylight, through denim,
the way we honor the art.
Nightfall and sunflower,
the way a bloodline is born.
Through parched grass, through violets,
think of the stitches —
melon rind, melon flesh,
I wrap our stories around me.
You stitch a plow's winding path
     when I board the train back,
loving turn of earth
     holding in, not keeping out.

     I leave Selma, filled
arms interlocked
with proof of fingers' work,
raising fences in honor.
How we weave love,
yield of crop,
into a soft, warming field.
Heart built on the strength of seed,
from the center out.

DRIVE-BY II: A SLIGHT RETURN

A carload of men speeds past me on the Hawkeye campus, screams
nigger & smiles, pleased in the deed
while rolling away.

I am alone,
just 12 years old, & this can't be
an act men are proud of.

OHIO RIVER/RIVER CITY (ALTERNATE TAKE)

Today, I laughed w/a friend,
said I'd come back to you
as a movie usher, reclaim
my high school job
just to count myself
among your suitors.

I'm not sure it was a joke.

That theater has come
& fled, a parking lot likely,
I don't know. I don't even venture
down that side of you anymore.
We could be lovers again, you
w/a head of brown current,
feet in Dixie. Me
in a sport coat (polyester blue),
the one I wore to tear tickets—
an eyesore
that would have balled me to flame
if any smoker
was two steps close.

I'm a sucker for romance,
but movies are artifice: camera,
lights & boom. Let me remove
my jacket, leave severed tickets
for the manager to count,
embrace your glass & corners—
cracks, missed lines & all.

THE SORROWS (A FRET IN THREE CHORDS)

I.

Each day, sun to borrowed sun, in hours of sweat & sorrow
Aligned as three stars, the belt of Orion, three brothers—
Duke, Buddy & Bo—stretch cracked hands to scorned earth,
Grab a heart's fill, Mr. Minter's dept the fly in ear, one
Bale the saving grace. How can six hands cover such tall orders?
Even tempered but hardly satisfied, they live in lack.

II.

Eluding pangs	of moonlight, hunger of night,	three men blood bound
Allow little rest,	limbs swing like hour, minute,	& second hands, flesh
Drawn through	spiked clouds at their ankles,	the pits of their stomachs
Growl in time	to work songs, the sun's lash.	The seeds inside the clouds,
Buddy says,	can work as feed scattered	for peck of beak. Minter's
Ether now,	bad dream floating, light	as a bale of cotton.

III.

End our toil in vain,	the rusted reigns	that clank a twelve-bar blues
Albeit an invisible	instrument. We	hunker in the shadow of sound
Divided in the map	of the row, one more	sack, full to feed the wicked
Gin, fast master	of commerce, tool	of chaos raised in wage of war
Buddy says fits	the best warlord.	Call him boss if you want, Buddy
Evokes another name:	face slap & upper	hand(s), black finger to fret.

SORGHUM

Once you hook mule to mill, you've married
the hours—worn the ring of stone's turn,
stalk grind, sugar pour. Marsh as sweet seed,
home of what stands tall, leans nervously
into living. You know all Mr. Minter wants
is cotton. Sorghum molasses—what you wish

could be poured over your cracked hands, ache
in the small of your back—ain't what white folks
crave. This your nigger consolation
only calloused & privileged could offer. Sugar,
not grains that make us whole.

†

There is a cotton field in Sardis, Alabama—
a stretch of mud & white
spread like the best patchwork—
before the church where Great Gran Matilda
was buried. After the service,
my kin walked aisles of puff & profit,
ushered samples back to bluegrass,
turned tufts between our fingers
to test the pain man made. I lost
that piece of cotton, raw resource
from the birth of my name, something
I can't get back unless I drive the miles,
see the South of my youth in a second
pilgrimage. When my days are done,
my words no longer barter, take me
there. Open the urn, spread my ashes
over evil's low fruit, let the burn stain
the ankle-high clouds, remind anyone
brave enough to walk the rows
how low a back must bend
to fill a sack
of sorrow.

III. \blak\ \al-fə bet\

"I am on I am on
I am pencilfrying
sweet Black alphabets
In an allnight oil"

— NIKKY FINNEY

PASSING NEGRO MOUNTAIN
(Garrett County, Maryland)

Admit it,

you read the title & thought
Here we go again—
another race poem,
(aren't we Post-black?)
or the word "Negro"
stuck its shackled ankle
in your path, reveled
@ the trip—thud . . .
or you asked *"Negro?"*
What century is this?
Perhaps, you laughed
at the way *Passing*
leaned into *N*, a hint
of identity intimacy,
the vacant trade
of dark for light.

    Imagine
being black, warring
w/red brothers, this mountain
the last place your chest
knows rise & fall . . .
warrior buried
in a hill to heaven, body
pushing bark
w/charcoal feet
to gun fire air.

. . . & the kicker,
in your long dead honor,
this bitter root:
the antiquated name.

INHABIT
(for Debra Kang Dean)

@ the podium, your fingers
find the page, flatten one's back
to another's stomach. The heel
of your hand stands north,

reverses the Great Migration.
Sometimes, you say, *women poets—*
poets of color—are called
to be spokespeople; I can't

even speak for myself.
One month prior,
a day of bloom & mirth,
you sign your first book—

a surprise—hand your words
across a congregation of emptied plates.
I mouth the inscription:
a silent sermon. Today,

the microphone
raises your slow breeze timbre,
praises the beat of your heart.
You are a patient ventriloquist:

your lips move & lyrics
float, bounce from speakers
hiding in walls. Your hand
moves again, an opening

to another room.
Heel of hand to page: rest,
slide, read, turn. Heel of hand
to page. Rest, slide.   Read.

THIS AFTERNOON,
KIRKWOOD AVENUE BREATHES

Behind the counter at the corner bookstore,
                            a woman sings Tori Amos—well.
Nose stud & outlined lips,
she arranges new porno mags
                    like the order matters.

I browse *Poets & Writers,*
                    search for salvation,
then retreat to the used bookstore
two doors down where two men
                            salivate for authors I don't know.

His mouth tired of praise,
one man hoists a box of hard covers,
quips, "I need another book
like I need a hole in my head."
                            We all could use that kind of space
I think, as I pick Natasha Trethewey
from a pile of paperbacks,
                    pretend not to eavesdrop.

TALLAHATCHIE
(for Emmett Till & Marilyn Nelson)

What are the odds?

One week after teaching Marilyn's crown
for Emmett, I crawl
on I-65 behind a white pickup
w/ Mississippi plates, the county
Tallahatchie.

For dramatic effect, it helps
we are witnessing a lightning
storm, two lanes narrow
to one, & I won't let anyone
cut between me
& the white truck.

The white lightning, I can't control.

I examine the contents
of the truck bed: tool box —
silver, textured; a cart upturned,
its wheels raised in surrender. No
cotton gin fans, no barbed wire
clues. Just my pen
scribbling in a Moleskine, a verse
for the dead, living
& mourning
@ 30 miles per hour.

The truck is the same race
as the driver & passenger—one
navigator, one witness—
same race as the student
who said, *This poem is racist,*
its continued references
to the word white are all negative
(Marilyn's not mine).

How the highway works:
speed, lines, a left
lane for passing
some barely driving—
or passing—never
leave. The classroom,
no safer.

LA OFRENDA

As poeta, I am sensitive
to certain truths: how
my verse sometimes falls
into a hammered riff of "b,"
how a short line
is a sharp line,
the mention of crimson
cliché. How names are poetry,
the rap of a family's honor
blessing the ear. Sometimes
the rhythm
is bitter.

What do you have to offer?

I bring these heightened senses
to an altar of remembrance.
Abuela—center of our earth—
we honor you
w/one tall burning candle,
black light, harvest moon;
a needle with unblocked eye,
thimble, fabric scraps
for patchwork magic; two bowls:
one of flour for the sustenance
you baked, the other
filled w/coffee beans
for the morning cup
you drank   deep.
        I could grind these dark cells,

mix the flour with buttermilk,
but they would not be your offerings,
another truth
I must bear.

       Forty-eight hours
before pencil-filled circles, our hand
feeding the machine
our dreams, El Dia
de los Muertos
will raise its skinless head
to laugh at the idea
of dying.
       Abuela,
can we honor the death
of a loveless effort:
the destruction of confidence,
violent mass, what weapons
a lie reveals? We wish
you were here to see us
add a bowl of oil
& a bullet
to la ofrenda, laugh
the blood of eight
away.

DRIVE-BY III: KIRKWOOD & GRANT

The initial slap of *nigger*,
the getaway grin. The way the word
reaches back through the smog
of a dragging muffler, slaps again.

IV. the book of names

"tell me your names, tell me your
bashful names and i will testify."

—LUCILLE CLIFTON

CERTIFICATE OF BIRTH
STATE OF ALABAMA—BUREAU OF VITAL STATISTICS

PLACE OF BIRTH

STATE BOARD OF HEALTH

County _Dallas_

Reg. District or
Beat No. _24 001 2_ Certificate No._____

Town or
City _Selma_

Street or
R.F.D._____ Ward_____
(If birth occurred in a hospital or institution, give its NAME instead of street and number)

Full Name of Child _Mamie Lee Johagan_

If child is not yet named, make
supplemental report when named.

| BOY OR / GIRL _girl_ | To be answered ONLY in event of plural births | 4 Twin, triplet or other_____ 5 Number, in order of birth_____ | (6) Are Parents Maried? _yes_ | (7)DATE OF BIRTH _Feb 9_ , 192 _4_ (Name of Month) (Day) (Year) |

FATHER		**MOTHER**	
FULL NAME _John Hardy Johagan_		(14) NAME BEFORE MARRIAGE _Matilda Holman_	
PRESENT POSTOFFICE OF FATHER _Tyler_		(15) PRESENT POSTOFFICE OF MOTHER _Tyler_	
COLOR OR RACE _colored_	(11) AGE AT LAST BIRTHDAY_____ (Years)	(16) COLOR OR RACE _colored_	(17) AGE AT LAST BIRTHDAY_____ (Years)
BIRTHPLACE _Dallas Co._		(18) BIRTHPLACE _Dallas Co._	
OCCUPATION _Farmer_		(19) OCCUPATION _Farm Wife_	
Number of children born to Mother, including present birth) _2_		(21) Number of children of this mother now living, including present birth) _2_	

CERTIFICATE OF ATTENDING PHYSICIAN OR MIDWIFE*

I hereby certify that I attended the birth of this child, who was born _alive_ at _8:45 a.m._
on the date above stated.   (Alive or Stillborn)   (Hour A.M. or P.M.)

(23) Signature _Julia Cohagan_
(24) State whether Physician or Midwife | _midwife_   (25) Address of Physician or Midwife _Tyler_

(26) Witness_____
(Signature of Witness necessary only when question 23 is signed by mark)

(27) Filed _Feb 23_ 192 _4_   (28) _Mrs E. Q. Pool_
Local Register

†

Turn w/me this book of names,
murmur of black skin
come & gone. Tell me

you've heard these names before,
exhaled o'er cane stalks,
sorghum, fields of lines

as midnight torch. I raise
each & every, 'til my hands
grow weak from weight, split

like silk before corn.
Everything buried, everything
birthed in earth,

something nurtured, watered
from parted rows.

Matilda
Leola
John
George
Mamie Lee
Mamie Lee
Mamie Lee

Amen.

PASSING NAMES

like brides lose their last,
gain a new, one worn

robe shed for next. This
we wear

threadbare. But
a nickname

passed from father to son?
The garment

untouched. Until
Buddy (Grandaddy)

has a boy, (Buddy),
& dreams

like parents do & dreams
sometimes undo &

son steps into a name
not stitched for him, ill

fit the fall of one.

WAR

calls sharecropper "sailor,"
trades sickle
for rifle, the grains
@ your back. The taste
of Leola's turnip greens
& tomatoes, orange juice
& Cocoa Cola, replaced
w/incessant rock . . . sonar . . .
so much blood. Wave & missile,
Fourth Fleet sifts Atlantic
for enemy. Once found,
guns weed U-boats faster
than a hoe blade crushes
boll weevils. Tongue heart-heavy,
there are many sights
George won't say. War
is not gossip
after discharge sends you home
to sit @ a table w/the woman
who will one day be your wife,
& all the limbs you waved
to say goodbye, the fear
@ your back.

OFFERINGS

Grandfather, 79, scales basement steps,
separates colors & whites
while you say *I can wash my own.*

Grandmother, 80, reads romance novels
like morning papers, sings gospel
with God's soul, hallowed notes.

Breakfast, toast points
pierce north, east & west,
George Washington, Mamie Lee & you.

Coffee instant, bacon fried long,
grits loose—a hard-boiled egg
rocks the edge of the grains.

Two smiles sip heat
from chipped cups, insist
you have seconds.

PASTOR'S NOTES: SUNDAY, MAY 8, 2005

BUS TRIP

Deposits for the Saturday, July 9 Guiding Star shopping excursion to Gatlinburg, Tenn., must be received in full by Sunday, May 15. The buses will leave promptly from the main church lot on 28th and Muhammad Ali Blvd. at 8 a.m. Please arrive early! No refunds will be given (yes, this includes those who miss the bus).

PASTOR'S ANNIVERSARY

Please join us on Sunday, June 19, for our annual Juneteenth/ Pastor's Anniversary celebration. Come celebrate Rev. & Mrs. Heard's 25 years of faithful leadership with a special Sunday worship service followed by the pastor's dinner in the church rectory hall. Donations to the Rev. & Mrs. Heard will be collected by the Women's Auxiliary.

SICK & SHUT-IN

Rev. Heard asks all members of Guiding Star Missionary Baptist Church to pray for our brothers and sisters who are unable to attend services this Sunday

†Georgia Arnold	†Mamie L. Green
†Antoine Bess	†J.D. Hunter
†April Brooks	†Nathaniel Mack
†Walter Campbell	†Cleophus Thomas
†Davis Frye	†Geraldine Watts

If you are able to phone or visit these members, please do so at your earliest convenience. Don't forget our church family. Even in absence, their spirit walks with us.

DOROTHY DRAWS BLOOD

Dorothy says, *This will sting a little*,
inserts the needle
before finishing
her sentence, never
gives you a chance
to wince.
      Seeing yourself
fill a vial with something warm,
sanguine, you can't help but wonder how
the body is measured.
           How
great a flood pumps the heart, sends
our veins humming ? What
moves valves to action, how
much lack makes us anemic? What if
when asked, regardless of whim, we can't
fill the clear?
      Understand,
we are soft machines: tender
at the mercy of age, silent
'til the moment
we are warned.

THE LETTING

If the needle pricks my finger
then it's alright—
gotta let a little blood
for the cotton. Watch it ride
down a cross stitch, resist
the urge to stay blue. Send my fingers
into holy throb, rifled pulse,
the thump of all
gone wrong. Let it go,
let it go, turn it tune
if you like. Makes no difference
if you can't sing, can't raise
the words.

      Can't tell me a needle
never lost its place,
felt more at home
in a hot skin pierce
than in anything
woven. Take your housetop
frame of gold, let it ripple
through every scattered scrap:
the threads you mend much sweeter
together. Map of our days,
a voice in every stab of thread,
my scarlet among the fabric,
kaleidoscope: family skin.

PATCHWORK

Missing her, I think
of first-stitch music,
the sound of cutting denim,

sheets & shirts
for a family's honored flag.
      When did she birth her vision?

Did it rise like waves of heat
from Sardis cotton fields, grow
from girl to woman

in dusty winds of unpaved paths
in Selma? Patchwork reminds me
of her hands, country-mile fingers,

masters of needle, thimble,
clink of dimpled metal
like castanets for Southern dances,

our partners poised
for one last spin.

TOWERS

Funny, near death
we are stacked

like the Passage: Treyton Oak,
Baptist . . . towers w/out

chains, floor after floor in wait
of the end of days. I hear

this is your life: East End, a tower
of wilt—too much to mourn

in one plot.
      You don't bound

down this street anymore.
Gait half slow drag/half pimp;

voice: well-bottom bark drummed
from pit of chest; face cloaked

in full beard; cast of eyes over horn-
rimmed glasses, down

at all as if looking through, always
looking. None of that now. Not

one scrap.
      Uncle,

do you know your mother's dead?
Do you have the heart to grieve?

Raise your sleeve, show me
the tuck has healed.

Just down Broadway—
nothing a TARC can't bridge—

but you feel an age
from us now, one long ride

of lonely, neither
black sheep nor scapegoat,

you are ghost—no presence
to blame or kick

& I am afraid
to raise your name.

THE ABSENCE OF MAMIE LEE

"Weep not, weep not, she is not dead;
she's resting in the bosom of Jesus."
James Weldon Johnson, "Go Down Death"

Thanksgiving, the first without you,
there are three pound cakes, none
close to your thick buttered sweet.

Momma, Aunt Cookie, Aunt Sissie,
all bake their version in tribute.
Still full from turkey & dressing,

we place the soft offerings
on the kitchen counter,
grab plates, forks & wait our turn.

     No one attempts to duplicate
your biscuits. Buttermilk,
flour, no measure—nothing

written to follow.
The cakes bring smiles,
but they are not yours,

& we keep tasting,
as if the more we eat,
the more we will remember.

Baking maps to the hereafter,
hoping one day to walk
the route.

SEMANTICS

She left you w/photo albums,
black & white souls
spilling from the pages between.
She left you with memories:
graduations, birthdays,
Sunday morning hat women
anchoring the front pew—
she being one; more
tattered squares, images
of an age before babies,
smiling friends caught
in the lens, a table
of empty bottles—
Pabst Blue Ribbon
Falls City—
glass monuments
to dance hall youth. She left you
an 80-year-old bachelor
w/ a nine-star constellation
& my crooked language.

Left you? Alone?
No,

but I wonder, grandfather,
after your bright stars
make phone calls,
whisk you away
to fried fish, black coffee,
& the hugs of grandchildren,

if you stand at the top step
& wave them down the driveway,
close the door to your silent house,
& sit in Grandma's wingback
with those swollen albums,
the totems falling.

Acknowledgements

Some of the poems in \blak\ \al-fə bet\ first appeared in the following journals and anthologies, sometimes in different versions:

Arable (Volume 1, Number 2, November 2004): "This Afternoon, Kirkwood Afternoon Breathes"
Callaloo (Volume 28 Number 4, Fall 2005): "Alabama, 1976"
Cave Canem XI: "Guiding Star Missionary Baptist Church (Rev. E. E. Heard, Pastor)
Crab Orchard Review (Fall 2007): "Inhabit"
Limestone (Fall 2011): "Bop: Ohio River/River City," "Semantics"
Reverie (Spring 2009): "Tallahatchie"
The Ringing Ear: Black Poets Lean South (2007, University of Georgia Press): "On the first drive-by"
Sou'wester (Fall 2010): "Coffer," "Patchwork"
Tidal Basin Review (2011): "Passing Negro Mountain," "Hood"
Zoland Poetry Vol. II (2008, Zoland Books): "Commandments," "Housetop"

The italicized passages in "Bop: Ohio River/River City" are lyrics from Radiohead's "Pyramid Song."

Blessings to the Affrilachian Poets; Cave Canem; the Kentucky Governor's School for the Arts; Indiana University-Purdue University Indianapolis; Indiana University Bloomington; Mom & Dad; George Washington Green (so many questions, thanks for your patience); John Green; Louisville, Ky. (West End. Yes.); Iowa City, Iowa; and Selma, Al. The places that raise you, never let you fall.

Analysis of Form: the Birth of the Fret

In the summer of 2010, the Affrilachian Poets (a coalition of poets of color from Appalachia) gathered in Chicago, Illinois, to celebrate the thirtieth birthday of our beloved sister, Parneshia Jones. In the midst of an elaborate barbecue (Parneshia's parents are famous for them), while drinking our favorite libation (bourbon), there was plenty of poetry. We were joined by friends Ed Roberson, Krista Franklin, Nicole Sealey, and others for a reading in the basement of Parneshia's parents' home (which, with its jukebox, bar, and dominoes games could give a real juke joint a run for its money any night). The energy of family and poetry led me to reveal a closely-guarded secret: for most of the summer, I had been working on a new form that would appear in my next collection—what eventually became \blak\ \al-fə bet\.

My plan was for the book to have a series of poems dedicated to the Alabama sharecropping days of my grandfather and his brothers, Milton and Sol. Right away, I was concerned with the danger in the familiar. Would I be accused of mining a subject that had been seen too often from a black poet? Did it matter? After all, this was the true history of my family.

I couldn't help but think of the criticism that a fellow Affrilachian Poet, Asha French, received during our MFA studies at Indiana University. After presenting a poem about lynching in workshop, a classmate responded "Everything about lynching worth reading was written in the Harlem Renaissance." (Somehow, I doubt anyone told Martha Collins that when she wrote *Blue Front*. If so, she obviously didn't listen.)

The creation of the Fret form (on pages TK of *blak*\ *al-fə bet*\) can be at least partially attributed to the anticipation the kind of criticism my friend received. Essentially, the form says, "Yes, you've heard about sharecropping, but have you heard it like this?" And *hearing* is key. To write the poems of my grandfather and his brothers working on the Minter plantation, I immersed myself in Son House and Skip James songs, hoping the blues could bind me emotionally to their sun up, sun down toil. I wasn't looking for the blues to define the external structure of the poems. Yet the heart of the blues is the guitar, so why not have a form that replicates the structure of the instrument?

In honor of the guitar's six strings, the Fret is six lines long. Each line begins with the letter of the corresponding guitar string as it appears on the neck from low note to high: EADGBE. Like strings, the lines are long and divided with aural and visual caesuras that mimic the separations of the guitar's fret board. Lastly, a poem written as a Fret must discuss struggle, meaning that, like any great story, a sense of conflict must be evident (a nod to the blues that are there in spirit, if not in formal design).

The more Frets I wrote, the more confident I became with the form. There was just one problem. Before I shared the form with my Affrilachian family, it didn't have a name. Once I shared it, the clear choice emerged. *Fret* had a nice ring to it, a quick clip of sound like the Bop, a form invented by the poet Afaa Michael Weaver, which we so admired. The name spoke to both the sense of struggle that is essential to the poem's internal structure and the physically divided appearance of its external structure. The name was natural, clever, and, most importantly, accurate. Thanks to Amanda Johnston for naming my creation.

It is my hope that, like the Bop, other poets take up the charge and experiment with this new form. That will ensure its longevity and, hopefully, do what I intended the invention of a new form to do: raise interest in this peculiar and beautiful obsession we call poetry.

—Mitchell L. H. Douglas,
Indianapolis, Indiana, December, 2011